BUILDING A BORDERLESS ECONOMY: THE NEXT STEP TOWARD GLOBAL UNITY

PROLOGUE

In a world increasingly defined by division, Embracing Humanity presented a radical vision: that cultural, national, and religious identities have long been the root of human suffering and must be transcended if we are to achieve genuine peace and progress. By discarding the boundaries that have separated us for centuries, we can create a future characterized by unity, empathy, and shared responsibility. Embracing Humanity laid out how rejecting cultural divisions and embracing a collective human identity could establish the foundation for addressing the global challenges that no nation can resolve alone.

In this book, Building a Borderless Economy: The Next Step Toward Global Unity, we extend that vision by exploring how we can transform our economic systems to reflect this shared human identity. If the previous book was about redefining who we are as a species, this book is about transforming how we live, work, and thrive together. A borderless economy represents the natural evolution of a world where borders no longer define us. It envisions a world where resources, opportunities, and prosperity are no longer hoarded by the few but shared by all. It is a world where we understand that the well-being of one is intrinsically tied to the well-being of all.

To fully appreciate the foundation on which this book is built, I encourage readers to begin with Embracing Humanity. That work provided the philosophical framework for a world beyond division; this book now offers a practical vision for constructing an economic system that supports that unity. Together, these two books form a comprehensive roadmap for how humanity can transcend the divisions of the past and build a world where everyone has the opportunity to flourish.

The journey toward a borderless world will not be easy, and it will require us to challenge deeply held beliefs about culture, sovereignty, and economic power. It will demand courage and a willingness to move beyond the familiar comforts of national identity and economic independence. Yet, I invite you to imagine what we could achieve by making these sacrifices—by prioritizing the collective good of humanity above all else, and by daring to create an interconnected world where we all rise together. Picture a future where prosperity, peace, and unity are not just ideals, but tangible realities accessible to everyone, everywhere, driven by our shared humanity and a commitment to leaving no one behind.

CHAPTER 1: INTRODUCTION: A BORDERLESS FUTURE

The idea of a borderless future may seem like a radical departure from the world we know today, but it is, in many ways, the logical evolution of humanity's progress. For centuries, borders have defined the contours of our existence—determining where we live, who we interact with, and how resources are distributed. Borders have served as symbols of sovereignty, expressions of identity, and mechanisms of control. Yet, they have also been sources of division, conflict, and inequality. The time has come to reimagine a world where borders no longer restrict our potential, where we can create a global community that prioritizes human flourishing over outdated notions of separation and exclusivity.

In Embracing Humanity, we explored the need to

transcend cultural, religious, and national identities in favour of a shared human identity—one that unites us all under a common banner of empathy and responsibility. This vision of a unified humanity is not merely an abstract ideal; it is a prerequisite for addressing the pressing challenges that face our world today. Climate change, pandemics, economic inequality, and social injustice do not respect borders. These are global issues that require global solutions, and the only way to achieve these solutions is through unity, cooperation, and the dismantling of artificial barriers that separate us.

This book, Building a Borderless Economy, takes that vision a step further by examining how our economic systems must evolve to support this new paradigm. The current global economic framework is inherently fragmented. Each nation operates within its own economic sphere, often prioritizing national interests at the expense of collective well-being. Trade policies, immigration restrictions, and protectionist measures all serve to maintain divisions that hinder the kind of global cooperation needed to tackle the most urgent issues of our time. A borderless economy seeks to change that by creating a system where resources, opportunities, and prosperity are shared equitably among all people, regardless of where they were born or what passport they hold.

Imagine a world where economic opportunity is not determined by geography. A world where a child born in a rural village in Africa has the same access to education, healthcare, and economic prospects as a child born in a major city in Europe or North America. This is not an impossible dream; it is a future that can be realized if we are willing to rethink the structures that have defined our economies for centuries. A borderless economy envisions a world where talent, innovation, and hard work are rewarded, not based on nationality, but based on the value they bring to humanity as a whole.

However, achieving this vision is not without its challenges. It will require a fundamental shift in the way we perceive sovereignty, economic power, and national interests. This transformation will not happen overnight, nor will it be without resistance. The concept of sovereignty has been deeply ingrained in our collective consciousness for centuries, and many will view any attempt to diminish national control as a threat to their identity and security. Yet, we must recognize that true security lies not in isolation but in cooperation and mutual support. The challenges we face today —whether environmental, economic, or social—are too vast and too interconnected to be solved by any one nation acting alone.

To move toward a borderless economy, we will need to create new global institutions and reform existing ones to better reflect our shared human values. Institutions such as the United Nations, the

World Trade Organization, and other international bodies must evolve to prioritize the collective well-being of humanity over the narrow interests of individual states. This means rethinking how we govern global trade, how we manage resources, and how we ensure that every person, regardless of nationality, has the opportunity to thrive. We will also need to establish mechanisms for global wealth redistribution to address the deep inequalities that exist between different regions of the world.

The role of technology in facilitating this transformation cannot be overstated. Advancements in digital infrastructure, blockchain, and artificial intelligence have the potential to create a more inclusive and equitable global economic system. Blockchain technology, for example, can provide transparency and security in financial transactions, reducing corruption and ensuring that resources are distributed fairly. Artificial intelligence can help optimize resource allocation, ensuring that food, water, and energy are directed where they are needed most. Digital platforms can connect people across borders, enabling collaboration and innovation on a scale never before possible. By leveraging these technologies, we can build an economic system that is not only efficient but also just and fair.

A borderless economy also requires a shift in our cultural values. We must move away from the idea that success is measured by the wealth of individual nations and toward a mindset that values the well-being of humanity as a whole. This means redefining what it means to be prosperous. Prosperity should not be about the accumulation of wealth by a select few, but about ensuring that every person has access to the resources they need to live a fulfilling life. It means prioritizing healthcare, education, and environmental sustainability over military spending and economic dominance. It means recognizing that the success of one individual or one community is intrinsically linked to the success of all.

The journey toward a borderless economy is not just about economic policy; it is about rethinking our values as a global society. It is about recognizing that the well-being of one person is intrinsically tied to the well-being of all. It is about understanding that in an interconnected world, the prosperity of one nation cannot come at the expense of another. By embracing a borderless future, we can create a world where prosperity, peace, and opportunity are available to everyone, everywhere. It is about creating a world where no one is left behind, where the talents and potential of every individual are recognized and nurtured, and where the barriers that have held us back for so long are finally dismantled.

This chapter will lay the foundation for the rest of the book by outlining the key concepts and ideas that will guide our exploration of a borderless economy. We will discuss why the current economic system is no longer sufficient for addressing the challenges of the 21st century, and how a new approach—one that transcends borders and embraces our shared humanity—can lead to a more just and sustainable world. We will delve into the practical steps needed to create this new economic reality, from establishing a global currency to implementing fair trade practices that ensure everyone benefits from the world's resources. As you read on, I invite you to consider what might be possible if we were to break free from the constraints of national borders and build an economy that works for all of us, not just the privileged few.

CHAPTER 2: THE PROBLEMS WITH THE CURRENT ECONOMIC SYSTEM

To understand why a borderless economy is necessary, we must first take a closer look at the fundamental flaws in the current global economic system. For centuries, our economic structures have been built around national borders, emphasizing national interests and reinforcing the inequalities that arise from differences in geography, wealth, and power. The world today is shaped by a fragmented system where each nation operates largely independently, often pursuing policies that benefit itself at the expense of others. This chapter will explore the limitations of this approach and illustrate why a new economic model is urgently needed.

The global economy is characterized by significant wealth inequality. A small number of wealthy nations hold the majority of the world's resources, while many developing countries struggle to meet the basic needs of their populations. This imbalance creates a cycle of poverty that is difficult to break. Countries rich in resources often exploit those with less, using their economic power to dictate terms that disproportionately benefit themselves. For example, during the colonial period and even in the modern era, many African countries rich in natural resources such as minerals and oil have found themselves at the mercy of powerful multinational corporations and wealthy nations. These nations and corporations often dictate terms that ensure the raw materials are extracted cheaply, while the profits are taken elsewhere, leaving the local populations with little economic benefit. This dynamic perpetuates a cycle where developing nations are unable to invest in infrastructure or education, keeping them reliant on foreign powers and unable to break free from poverty. These dynamics perpetuate a system of exploitation and inequity that prevents many people from achieving a reasonable standard of living, let alone thriving.

This inequality is further compounded by trade policies and immigration restrictions. Wealthy nations frequently impose trade barriers that limit the ability of developing countries to compete in the global market. Tariffs, subsidies, and quotas are all tools used to protect domestic industries, but they often come at the expense of developing nations that cannot afford to play by the same rules. The current system rewards those who are already economically powerful while systematically disadvantaging those who are trying to improve their circumstances. Immigration policies also play a role in maintaining inequality. The movement of people across borders is restricted, limiting the ability of individuals to seek out better opportunities and improve their lives. In a world where some nations have an abundance of resources and others face scarcity, these restrictions only serve to deepen the divide.

Another critical problem with the current economic system is its emphasis on competition over cooperation. National economies are largely driven by the pursuit of self-interest—nations seek to maximize their own wealth, often without regard for the well-being of others. This competitive mindset has led to a world where nations are pitted against each other in a zero-sum game, vying for control over resources, markets, and influence. This competition fuels conflict, destabilizes regions, and ultimately hinders our ability to address the challenges that face us all. Climate change, for instance, requires a unified, global response, yet national interests often prevent meaningful progress. Countries are reluctant to make sacrifices that might disadvantage them economically, even if those sacrifices are essential for the collective well-being of humanity.

The current economic system also fails to address the challenges of the 21st century. As we face an increasingly interconnected world, issues such as climate change, global health crises, and technological disruption cannot be effectively managed by nations acting in isolation. The COVID-19 pandemic provided a stark illustration of this point. While some nations were able to mobilize resources to protect their citizens, others were left to fend for themselves, lacking the infrastructure, funding, and international support necessary to respond effectively. The pandemic highlighted the weaknesses of a fragmented global system and underscored the need for coordinated action that transcends borders. A borderless economic system would allow us to pool resources, share information, and act collectively to address such challenges.

The economic system we have today also places profit above people. Corporations, driven by the imperative to maximize shareholder returns, often exploit workers, degrade the environment, and ignore the social impact of their actions. This profit-driven mentality leads to practices that are harmful to both individuals and communities, particularly in developing nations where labour and environmental protections are weaker. The pursuit of profit at any cost has also contributed significantly to environmental degradation. The extraction of natural resources, pollution, and the disregard for environmental limits are all by-products of an economic system that values short-term gain over long-term sustainability. This model is simply not compatible with the needs of a planet facing a climate crisis.

One of the most glaring flaws in the current system is the lack of a social safety net that ensures basic economic security for all individuals. Economic downturns, job losses, and health crises can leave individuals and families in desperate situations with no support. This is where the idea of a minimum living wage becomes crucial. By providing a guaranteed income to every working-age citizen—regardless of employment status—we can ensure that everyone has a foundation upon which to build a better future. Such a system would provide stability for those between jobs, support individuals who wish to pursue further education or personal development and reduce the anxiety that comes from living paycheck to paycheck. A minimum living wage would also serve as an important supplement for those who are employed but still struggle to make ends meet. In a world that prioritizes human well-being over profit, ensuring that everyone has access to the basic necessities of life is a fundamental requirement.

The flaws in the current economic system are clear: inequality, competition over cooperation, profit-driven exploitation, and a lack of basic economic security. These issues are not just unfortunate byproducts of our economic model—they are intrinsic to its design. A system that prioritizes national interests, corporate profits, and the accumulation of wealth by a select few will always leave many people behind. It will always create divisions, fuel conflict, and hinder our collective progress. Inequality will continue to rise, as the gap between the wealthy and the impoverished widens, perpetuating social unrest and limiting opportunities for countless individuals. The very fabric of our society becomes strained when basic needs are not met, and the promise of a better life remains out of reach for so many.

The competition-centric mindset that underpins our current economic systems encourages nations and corporations to prioritize their own short-term gains over the long-term well-being of the global population. This competitive approach ultimately erodes the spirit of collective human progress. When each nation is striving solely for its own success, international cooperation is seen as optional rather than essential. This lack of collaboration prevents us from addressing the global challenges that require coordinated responses, such as climate change, pandemics, and poverty.

Moreover, the emphasis on profit-driven exploitation means that environmental degradation and human suffering are treated as acceptable trade-offs in the pursuit of economic growth. Corporations that prioritize profit over people often contribute to the depletion of natural resources, pollution, and exploitative labour practices, which further marginalize already vulnerable populations. This relentless pursuit of profit leads to the externalization of costs—meaning the most disadvantaged communities pay the price for the actions of those at the top.

A system that lacks basic economic security for its citizens is destined to create a precarious existence for many. Without a safety net, people are left vulnerable to economic shocks, health crises, and other unforeseen events. The lack of support leads to cycles of poverty that become increasingly difficult to escape. In contrast, a system that guarantees a minimum living wage would offer the stability necessary for individuals to invest in their futures, pursue education, and contribute meaningfully to society. Such stability is not just a matter of economic policy; it is a fundamental human right that ensures dignity and opportunity for all.

To move beyond these limitations, we need a new approach—one that transcends borders, values cooperation over competition, and puts the well-being of humanity at the centre of all economic activity. This new system must be built on principles of equity, sustainability, and shared prosperity. It requires a reimagining of what it means to succeed—not just for individuals or nations, but for humanity as a whole. We must strive for an economy where resources are allocated based on need and where opportunities are not confined by geography, nationality, or social status.

The vision of a borderless economy is one in which resources are shared, opportunities are available to all, and no one is left behind. It is an economy that recognizes the interconnectedness of our world and the fact that the challenges we face—whether environmental, social, or economic—can only be solved through collective action. A borderless economy represents not just an economic transformation but a moral one, where we recognize our responsibilities to each other and to future generations. It envisions a world where the value of a person is not measured by their wealth or nationality but by their humanity and potential.

The next chapter will explore how we can begin to dismantle the barriers that prevent us from achieving this vision and what steps are necessary to build a global economic system that works for everyone. As we move forward, let us remember that the well-being of one is intrinsically tied to the well-being of all, and that by working together, we can create a world where prosperity, peace, and opportunity are not privileges enjoyed by the few, but rights guaranteed to all. This will require a fundamental shift in our thinking—from seeing ourselves as isolated actors in a competitive landscape to understanding ourselves as members of a shared global community, united by our common humanity and our collective aspirations for a better future.

CHAPTER 3: ECONOMIC INEQUALITY AND THE NEED FOR A GLOBAL APPROACH

One of the most pressing challenges humanity faces today is the pervasive issue of economic inequality. The disparity between the wealthy and the poor is widening, creating significant barriers for millions of people who are struggling to improve their quality of life. Economic inequality not only affects individuals but also erodes the social fabric, fuels conflict and hinders global progress. If we are to create a future that works for everyone, we must adopt a global approach that addresses the root causes of inequality and ensures that opportunities are available to all, regardless of where they live.

Economic inequality can be understood as the unequal distribution of resources, wealth, and opportunities among individuals and nations. This disparity is often stark: on one side, we have countries and individuals who enjoy vast wealth, access to high-quality healthcare, education, and the opportunity to shape their futures; on the other side, millions of people live without even the most basic necessities. For instance, according to Oxfam, the world's richest 1% possess more wealth than the rest of the global population combined. This statistic speaks to the extreme concentration of wealth at the top and highlights the systemic imbalances that keep billions in poverty.

Economic inequality is deeply linked to geographic disparities. Many nations, particularly in sub-Saharan Africa, face significant challenges related to poverty, infrastructure, education, and healthcare. These challenges are often perpetuated by colonial legacies, which left newly independent nations with weak economic foundations, unbalanced trade relationships, and a lack of investment in local industries. For example, many African nations still rely heavily on exporting raw materials, such as minerals and agricultural products, which often have lower profit margins compared to the finished goods produced by wealthier countries. As a result, these nations remain at the mercy of fluctuating global markets, limiting their ability to build strong and diverse economies.

Addressing economic inequality requires global institutions to play a more proactive role. Institutions like the United Nations, the World Bank, and the International Monetary Fund (IMF) have historically worked to address global poverty through development programs, loans, and aid. However, these efforts have often fallen short, as they tend to focus on short-term solutions without addressing the systemic issues that perpetuate inequality. In many cases, IMF loans have come with conditions that force borrowing nations to implement austerity measures, reducing public spending on essential services such as healthcare and education. These measures often exacerbate poverty rather than alleviate it.

A more effective approach would involve reforming these global institutions to prioritize sustainable development and human well-being over economic growth metrics. For example, rather than focusing solely on increasing GDP, the World Bank could emphasize reducing poverty rates, improving access to education, and ensuring that healthcare is available to all. Moreover, global institutions should facilitate fair trade agreements that allow developing countries to retain more of the value generated by their natural resources. An example of this would be renegotiating trade deals to ensure that nations exporting raw materials receive a fair share of the profits, which could then be reinvested in infrastructure, education, and social services.

Redistribution of wealth is a crucial component of addressing economic inequality. While redistribution has often been framed as a national issue—where governments use taxes and social programs to balance wealth within their borders—it must also be considered at a global level. The world today is more interconnected than ever before, and the actions of wealthy nations and multinational corporations have direct consequences on the economic well-being of people in other parts of the world.

An example of this can be seen in the realm of tax avoidance. Many multinational corporations use tax havens to avoid paying taxes in the countries where they generate significant profits. This deprives developing nations of the revenue needed to fund public services, such as healthcare and education. In 2021, it was estimated that around $427 billion in taxes is lost globally every year due to corporate tax avoidance. If these funds were made available to the countries where they were earned, they could be used to lift millions out of poverty and reduce inequality on a significant scale.

Another essential aspect of reducing global economic inequality is the implementation of a minimum living wage for all working-age individuals. Unlike traditional welfare systems, which are often means-tested and targeted, a minimum living wage would provide a guaranteed income to everyone, regardless of their employment status. This would not only help to alleviate poverty but also provide economic stability for those between jobs, or those who wish to pursue education and skill development without the immediate pressure of earning a living.

Consider the example of Universal Basic Income (UBI) pilot projects that have been conducted in various parts of the world. In Finland, a two-year UBI experiment provided unemployed citizens with a monthly payment of 560 euros, regardless of whether they found work. The results indicated that participants reported higher levels of well-being, reduced stress, and greater opportunities to pursue job training or other productive activities. Although UBI is not the same as a minimum living wage, the concept of providing a basic income to all citizens has shown promising results in improving economic security and reducing inequality.

A global minimum living wage would ensure that everyone, regardless of where they live, has a foundation upon which to build a better life. It would also reduce the economic pressures that force individuals into exploitative labour conditions or prevent them from pursuing education and entrepreneurship. By providing a safety net for all, we can create a more resilient global economy where everyone has the opportunity to thrive.

To address economic inequality, we must also reimagine the way we trade and distribute resources. The current system often favours wealthy nations that have the power to dictate the terms of trade, leaving poorer countries at a disadvantage. Fair trade practices aim to correct this imbalance by ensuring that producers in developing countries receive fair compensation for their goods, which allows them to reinvest in their communities and improve their standard of living.

An example of successful fair-trade initiatives can be seen in the coffee industry. Fairtrade-certified coffee cooperatives in Latin America have provided small-scale farmers with better prices for their beans, access to global markets, and the ability to invest in their farms and communities. This has not only improved the economic well-being of farmers but also contributed to social development, as profits are often used to fund schools, healthcare facilities, and infrastructure projects. Expanding fair trade practices to other industries and regions can help create a more equitable global economy where all participants benefit.

Technology also has a critical role to play in reducing economic inequality. Digital platforms can provide access to financial services for the unbanked, enable remote learning for those without access to traditional educational institutions, and create opportunities for individuals to participate in the global economy. For instance, mobile banking services like M-Pesa in Kenya have revolutionized the way people access financial services, allowing millions of previously unbanked individuals to save money, access credit, and participate in commerce. This type of technological innovation has the potential to reduce the gap between the wealthy and the poor by providing opportunities that were previously inaccessible.

Another example is the rise of online education platforms, such as Coursera and edX, which offer courses from top universities to people around the world, often for free or at a low cost. These platforms allow individuals in developing countries to acquire skills and knowledge that can help them improve their economic prospects. By leveraging technology to break down barriers to education and financial inclusion, we can create a more equitable world where opportunities are not limited by geography or socioeconomic status.

Addressing economic inequality requires a fundamental shift in the way we think about wealth, resources, and opportunity. It requires us to move beyond the notion that economic success is a zero-sum game, where one nation's gain is another's loss. Instead, we must embrace the idea that global prosperity benefits everyone, and that reducing inequality is essential for creating a stable, peaceful, and thriving world.

A borderless economy, one that prioritizes human well-being over national interests, is the key to addressing the root causes of economic inequality. By working together, reforming global institutions, ensuring fair trade, implementing a minimum living wage, and leveraging technology, we can create a world where everyone has the opportunity to succeed. This chapter has laid out the key elements of a global approach to reducing economic inequality. The next chapter will explore how we can move toward establishing a global currency that facilitates equitable trade and economic stability for all.

As we move forward, let us remember that economic inequality is not an inevitability—it is a consequence of the choices we make as a society. By choosing to adopt a global perspective, prioritize fairness, and invest in the well-being of all people, we can create a future where economic opportunity is not a privilege for the few, but a right for all.

CHAPTER 4: TOWARD A UNIFIED GLOBAL CURRENCY

As we work towards creating a borderless economy, one crucial aspect that must be addressed is the concept of a unified global currency. The idea of a single global currency has long been a subject of debate, with supporters arguing that it could lead to greater economic stability, easier trade, and equitable growth, while detractors raise concerns about the loss of national sovereignty and potential economic risks. In this chapter, we explore why a unified global currency is a necessary step for building an interconnected world that transcends borders, reduces inequalities, and enables a more resilient and cooperative global economy.

Today, the world operates on a diverse and often fragmented monetary system. Each nation has its own currency, which is backed by its own economic policies, stability, and resources. The differences between currencies create significant challenges for global trade, as fluctuations in exchange rates can have a profound impact on the value of imports and exports, complicate financial planning for businesses, and create risks for investors. These challenges are further exacerbated by the uncertainty that exchange rate fluctuations introduce into international trade agreements, making long-term contracts riskier and often leading to hesitancy in cross-border investments. For small and medium enterprises, the costs of managing currency risk can be prohibitive, limiting their ability to participate in international markets and stifling innovation and growth.

These fluctuations often have a disproportionate effect on developing countries, whose economies are more vulnerable to global market shifts. In developing nations, currency depreciation can lead to skyrocketing prices for essential goods, disproportionately impacting low-income populations and worsening inequality. Additionally, many of these countries rely heavily on foreign-denominated loans to finance infrastructure projects and other critical investments. When their currencies lose value, the cost of servicing these debts increases, putting immense pressure on already strained public finances. This cycle of currency instability and debt burden can trap countries in a vicious cycle of poverty, unable to invest in social services or economic development initiatives that could improve the well-being of their populations.

Moreover, the fragmented nature of the current monetary system means that nations must maintain significant foreign exchange reserves to manage their currencies and defend against speculative attacks. This ties up valuable resources that could otherwise be used for development projects, education, healthcare, or other areas that directly benefit citizens. A unified global currency could alleviate these burdens, freeing up resources for more productive uses and allowing countries to focus on growth and development rather than currency management and defence. By creating a stable, predictable economic environment, a unified currency could help bridge the gap between developed and developing nations, fostering a more inclusive global economy where all nations can thrive.

For instance, during times of global economic instability, currency devaluation can make it exceedingly difficult for countries to pay for essential imports, such as food and medicine, leading to severe humanitarian consequences. The 1997 Asian Financial Crisis is an example of how currency instability can devastate entire regions. The crisis started when the Thai baht collapsed, setting off a chain reaction that led to a massive outflow of capital from other Asian economies, causing widespread unemployment and poverty. In Indonesia, for example, the crisis caused the value of the rupiah to plummet, leading to skyrocketing inflation that made basic goods unaffordable for millions of people. The effects were felt for years, with the economic downturn leading to widespread malnutrition, increased poverty rates, and political instability. Such economic disruptions highlight the vulnerabilities that exist within the current monetary framework, particularly for developing nations that lack the economic resilience to weather such shocks. The crisis also underscored the interconnected nature of modern economies—when one nation faced a financial collapse, the ripple effects spread rapidly, demonstrating that currency instability is not a problem confined within national borders but a global issue requiring a coordinated response. Addressing these challenges through a unified global currency could help mitigate the risks of such crises, providing a stable economic foundation that benefits all nations, especially those most vulnerable.

The complexity of dealing with multiple currencies also creates barriers for small businesses and entrepreneurs who want to enter the global market. Large multinational corporations often have the resources to hedge against currency risk and navigate complex international banking systems, but smaller businesses do not. This lack of access further exacerbates economic inequality, as it prevents many individuals from benefiting from global trade opportunities. Entrepreneurs in developing countries are often unable to expand beyond their local markets because they lack the resources to manage foreign currency risks, limiting their potential for growth and the economic prosperity of their communities.

A unified global currency could solve many of these problems by eliminating exchange rate fluctuations, reducing transaction costs, and providing a more stable economic environment for all countries—especially those currently disadvantaged by the volatility of the existing system. The removal of currency exchange barriers would make it significantly easier for small businesses to participate in international trade, thereby fostering inclusive economic growth and narrowing the gap between the wealthy and the poor.

A unified global currency offers several significant benefits that align with the vision of a borderless economy. One of the most important advantages is the potential for economic stability. By eliminating currency fluctuations, countries could engage in trade without the fear of sudden devaluations or adverse effects from shifts in foreign exchange markets. This stability would enable more predictable and sustainable growth, benefiting both businesses and individuals. Without the challenges of fluctuating exchange rates, businesses would be better able to plan for the future, make long-term investments, and expand their operations globally. This would, in turn, create more jobs, stimulate innovation, and enhance overall productivity.

Furthermore, economic stability brought by a unified currency could help prevent financial crises that are often triggered by volatile currency markets. In times of economic uncertainty, countries currently face significant risks from speculative attacks on their currencies, which can lead to rapid devaluations and economic turmoil. A unified currency would remove this vulnerability, providing a safeguard against the kind of financial instability that has plagued many nations in the past. For individuals, this means a more secure financial environment where savings retain their value, and the cost of living remains stable.

The potential for stable and predictable economic growth would also make it easier for governments to focus on long-term social and economic policies rather than constantly reacting to short-term financial shocks. This would allow for greater investment in infrastructure, healthcare, education, and other sectors that are crucial for improving the quality of life for citizens. The benefits of stability would extend beyond purely economic metrics, fostering a society where people have greater confidence in their future and the future of their children.

Ultimately, the introduction of a unified global

currency could serve as a powerful tool for reducing poverty and inequality. By creating a stable economic environment, countries could focus on equitable growth and sustainable development, ensuring that the benefits of globalization reach everyone. This shift could help bridge the gap between wealthy and poorer nations, allowing for a more inclusive global economy that provides opportunities for all.

Another key benefit of a global currency is the reduction in transaction costs. Today, individuals and businesses pay substantial fees when converting one currency to another. These costs can add up, particularly for businesses that engage in frequent international trade. A unified currency would eliminate these costs, making global commerce more efficient and accessible. For consumers, it would mean more affordable goods and services, as the costs of currency conversion and financial transactions would no longer need to be passed along in the form of higher prices. The removal of these additional costs would make everyday purchases more accessible to people across all income levels, significantly enhancing their purchasing power and improving their quality of life. The cumulative effect of these reduced costs could lead to significant gains in economic efficiency and consumer welfare, as more resources would be available for productive use rather than being wasted on unnecessary financial fees. For small businesses, this reduction in transaction costs could make the difference between success and failure, as lower costs would enable them to compete more effectively in international markets. With increased competition, consumers would also benefit from lower prices and a wider variety of goods and services. Additionally, eliminating these costs would remove a major barrier to entry for entrepreneurs in developing countries, fostering greater economic participation and growth. The cumulative impact of these changes would contribute to a more dynamic, inclusive, and prosperous global economy, where economic opportunities are more evenly distributed, and the benefits of globalization are felt by all.

A unified global currency would also enhance economic equity. Currently, countries with weaker currencies face significant disadvantages in the global market. Their exports are often undervalued, and they must pay more for imports, creating an imbalance that is difficult to overcome. This imbalance creates a cycle of poverty that is hard to break, as the weaker economies are constantly at a disadvantage when trying to compete with wealthier nations. A global currency would level the playing field, ensuring that all countries participate in trade on equal terms. By removing the systemic bias that favours stronger currencies, we can help developing nations grow and thrive, leading to greater global prosperity. This would not only benefit developing nations but also contribute to global economic stability, as disparities in wealth and opportunity are often the root causes of conflict and instability.

A unified currency would also ensure that developing nations can attract foreign investment on fairer terms. Currently, investors often view currency volatility as a significant risk, which leads them to demand higher returns or avoid investing altogether in countries with weaker currencies. With a single global currency, the risk associated with currency fluctuations would be eliminated, making developing nations more attractive to investors. This increased flow of investment could be used to build infrastructure, improve healthcare and education, and support local businesses, leading to long-term economic growth and prosperity.

Moreover, a global currency would reduce the influence of speculative attacks that disproportionately harm weaker economies. Speculators often target currencies they perceive as vulnerable, leading to rapid devaluations and economic crises that can set back progress for years or even decades. By eliminating the possibility of such speculative attacks, a unified currency would provide a much-needed safety net for countries that have historically been the most vulnerable to external financial shocks. This would allow these nations to focus on internal development rather than constantly having to react to external financial pressures.

Additionally, the elimination of currency barriers would promote inclusive trade and allow developing nations to have more control over their economic destinies. Currently, the financial systems and currency dynamics favour wealthier countries, which can afford to manipulate their monetary policies to maintain an advantageous position in the global market. A unified currency would take away this advantage, ensuring that all nations start on more equal footing. This would be particularly beneficial for emerging economies that need fair access to international markets to achieve their potential. By levelling the playing field, we can create a world where the progress of a nation is not hindered by arbitrary financial disadvantages.

By fostering such an environment, a unified global currency would not only help developing nations but would also benefit the entire world by creating a more stable and resilient global economy. Economic stability and equity across all nations would mean fewer economic shocks and crises, which often have ripple effects that impact even the most economically secure countries. This holistic approach to economic development would contribute to a more peaceful and cooperative international community, as countries would no longer be pitted against each other in a battle for economic dominance. Instead, they would be united in their efforts to ensure collective prosperity and well-being.

One of the primary concerns raised by opponents of a unified global currency is the potential loss of national sovereignty. Currency is often seen as a symbol of a nation's independence, and giving up control over monetary policy can be perceived as a loss of self-determination. However, as argued in our previous book, we envision a future in which global governance replaces the fragmented systems that currently divide humanity. In this future, nations would no longer need to see themselves as isolated entities competing for resources and power, but rather as part of a larger human community committed to shared well-being.

The move to a unified global currency would require global financial institutions to take on a greater role in managing monetary policy. This would involve establishing mechanisms for ensuring that all nations have a voice in decision-making and that policies are designed to promote equity and sustainability rather than serving the interests of a select few powerful economies. Such an approach would be consistent with the vision of a global government, where taxes and resources are collected centrally and redistributed to ensure the well-being of all people, regardless of where they live. By centralizing financial authority under a global institution that represents the interests of all nations equally, we can create a system that is both fair and effective in promoting the economic prosperity of all citizens of the world.

The creation of the Euro provides a valuable historical example of how a unified currency can promote economic integration. Before the Euro, European nations faced many of the same challenges that exist globally today—currency fluctuations, trade barriers, and economic inequalities between member states. The adoption of the Euro eliminated these barriers and has helped to create a more integrated and stable European economy. The Euro has made trade easier, lowered transaction costs, and strengthened the economic ties between member nations, reducing the likelihood of conflict and fostering cooperation.

However, the Euro is not without its challenges. The European debt crisis of the early 2010s highlighted the difficulties of managing a single currency across multiple nations with different economic policies and levels of development. The crisis underscored the importance of cohesive fiscal policies and the need for solidarity between member nations. These lessons must be taken into account when designing a global currency to ensure that it benefits all participants and that mechanisms are in place to support countries facing economic difficulties. A unified global currency would require stronger mechanisms for fiscal coordination, as well as safeguards to ensure that economically weaker nations are not left behind in times of crisis.

The creation of a unified global currency would require careful planning and the establishment of strong global institutions to manage it. A new Global Central Bank could be established, responsible for issuing the currency, managing monetary policy, and ensuring economic stability. This institution would need to be democratic, with representation from all nations to ensure that the interests of both developed and developing countries are considered.

A unified currency would also require the adoption of common economic standards and regulations to prevent imbalances and ensure fair participation. This means creating mechanisms for wealth redistribution, much like how taxes are collected by national governments today and used to fund social services. In a global context, taxes would be collected centrally by the global government and redistributed to support infrastructure, healthcare, education, and social welfare programs in all regions, particularly those that have been historically disadvantaged. This centralization of wealth and resource management would help reduce economic disparities and ensure that every nation has the support needed to thrive.

To ease the transition to a unified global currency, a phased approach could be adopted. Initially, countries could voluntarily peg their currencies to the new global standard, creating greater stability without immediately abandoning their national currencies. Over time, as trust in the new system grows and the benefits become clear, countries could gradually transition to using the global currency exclusively. This phased approach would help minimize disruption and allow nations to adapt to the new system at a pace that suits their economic realities.

A unified global currency has the potential to foster economic resilience by encouraging nations to work together to address economic challenges. When countries share a common currency, their fates are more closely intertwined, creating a powerful incentive to cooperate rather than compete. This interconnectedness would make it easier to implement global economic policies aimed at addressing climate change, pandemics, and technological disruptions—challenges that no single nation can solve alone. A unified currency would provide the financial stability needed to invest in long-term solutions to these pressing issues, benefiting the entire global community.

By reducing the barriers to trade and creating a more equitable economic environment, a unified global currency could also encourage entrepreneurship and innovation. With fewer financial obstacles, individuals and businesses would have greater opportunities to enter new markets, collaborate across borders, and contribute to global progress. This would lead to a more dynamic and inclusive global economy, where the benefits of growth are shared by all. Entrepreneurs from developing nations would have the same access to international markets as those from wealthier countries, enabling them to innovate, grow, and contribute to the global economy on equal footing.

A unified global currency is a critical component of building a borderless economy that works for everyone. By eliminating the barriers created by multiple currencies, we can create a more stable, equitable, and resilient economic system that benefits all nations and people. While the transition to a global currency will undoubtedly be challenging, the potential rewards—greater stability, reduced inequality, and enhanced global cooperation—make it a goal worth pursuing.

The vision of a world united by a single currency aligns with the broader goals of global governance and shared human identity that we have discussed in my previous book. By adopting a unified currency, we can take an important step toward creating a world where economic opportunity is not determined by geography, where cooperation replaces competition, and where the well-being of all people is prioritized over the interests of a few.

CHAPTER 5: GLOBAL TAXATION AND RESOURCE REDISTRIBUTION

In the pursuit of a unified world, the concept of global taxation and resource redistribution becomes essential. A truly borderless economy requires that resources be shared equitably, ensuring that every human being, regardless of nationality, has access to a minimum standard of living. This chapter will discuss how global taxation could work in practice, the principles behind it, and how such a system could help address the disparities that have long defined our world. By ensuring that wealth and resources are redistributed on a global scale, we can create a foundation for shared prosperity, making it possible for everyone to benefit from the fruits of progress.

In our current economic system, wealth inequality is pervasive both within and between nations. While some countries enjoy enormous prosperity, others struggle to provide even the most basic services to their citizens. This inequality creates instability, fosters resentment, and impedes global cooperation. A system of global taxation would address these disparities by collecting resources centrally and ensuring they are redistributed to meet the needs of all people, regardless of where they are born.

Global taxation should be universal and replace all existing taxes, with all revenue being paid directly to a global government. This means that individual nations would no longer collect taxes for their own purposes; instead, all taxation would be consolidated under a global system designed to benefit humanity as a whole. Such an approach would eliminate the inefficiencies of fragmented national tax systems and ensure that resources are distributed according to global needs rather than national interests.

The idea of global taxation is not new, but it has often been met with resistance due to concerns over national sovereignty. Many nations are hesitant to give up control over their tax systems, fearing that doing so would compromise their independence. However, as we have argued throughout this book, the challenges facing humanity today are too vast and interconnected to be addressed by individual nations acting alone. A system of global taxation would replace national tax systems entirely, ensuring that resources are used to address the needs of all people, rather than being hoarded by individual countries. This kind of cooperation is essential for tackling issues like climate change, pandemics, and global poverty—challenges that no one nation can solve on its own.

The implementation of a global tax system would require the creation of a Global Revenue Authority, a body responsible for collecting and distributing taxes on a worldwide scale. This institution would need to be representative of all nations, ensuring that the voices of both developed and developing countries are heard. The Global Revenue Authority would be tasked with establishing tax rates, collecting revenue, and ensuring that funds are distributed equitably based on need. It would also be responsible for ensuring transparency and accountability, so that all nations can trust that the resources they contribute are being used effectively and fairly.

Under this system, all forms of taxation—whether on income, wealth, or corporate profits—would be standardized and administered by the global government. This would eliminate the inefficiencies and inequalities that arise from having different tax rates and rules across countries. The progressive nature of the tax system would ensure that those with the greatest ability to pay contribute the most. A progressive wealth tax would ensure that the wealthiest individuals and corporations contribute a fair share to support global development. This approach could help bridge the gap between the rich and the poor, both within and between nations, creating a more equitable global society.

A global corporate tax would be levied on multinational corporations, ensuring that they contribute fairly to the global economy from which they profit. This tax would address the growing disparity between corporations that reap enormous benefits from globalization and the communities that often face the negative impacts of their operations. By establishing a standardized global corporate tax rate, the system would prevent corporations from exploiting tax havens and other loopholes that allow them to minimize their tax obligations unfairly. The revenue generated from this tax could be used to fund global development projects, improve infrastructure in underdeveloped areas, and ensure that all nations benefit from corporate profits. This global corporate tax would help level the playing field, allowing smaller economies to thrive without being undermined by the power and influence of large multinational corporations. By enforcing fair contributions from the wealthiest and most profitable companies, we can foster an economic environment where businesses are encouraged to invest in communities, create jobs, and support sustainable practices that benefit the entire world.

Another potential component of a global tax system is a carbon tax. Climate change is one of the most pressing challenges facing humanity, and it requires a coordinated global response. A carbon tax would place a price on activities that contribute to greenhouse gas emissions, providing a strong incentive for businesses and individuals to reduce their carbon footprint. The revenue generated from a global carbon tax could be used to fund renewable energy projects, support communities affected by climate change, and help developing nations transition to more sustainable forms of energy. The hope is that with effective global coordination, innovation, and cooperation, we could reach a point where climate change is effectively managed, and the need for such a tax diminishes over time. By investing in green infrastructure, supporting technological advancements, and fostering a culture of sustainability, we could create a world where the threats posed by climate change are proactively addressed, making punitive measures like carbon taxes eventually obsolete. This vision of a united, cooperative approach to tackling climate change can also serve as a model for addressing other global challenges, highlighting the power of collective action in achieving lasting solutions.

The revenue collected through global taxation would be used to fund resource redistribution on a global scale. This redistribution would focus on ensuring that every human being has access to the basic necessities of life—food, clean water, healthcare, education, and shelter. By providing a minimum standard of living for all people, we can create a foundation upon which individuals can build better lives for themselves and their families.

Revenue collected would also be used to fund the universal basic wage, providing a consistent and reliable source of income for all citizens, regardless of their employment status. This universal basic wage would serve not only as a safety net for those who are unable to find work, but also as a means of empowering individuals to take risks, pursue entrepreneurial ventures, or focus on education and skills development without the fear of financial instability. By ensuring that everyone has a basic level of financial security, we can create an environment where people are free to innovate, invest in their future, and contribute positively to their communities. The universal basic wage would be a cornerstone of a fairer society, where economic opportunities are available to all, and where the fear of destitution is eliminated, allowing for a more motivated, healthy, and productive global population.

In addition to meeting basic needs, resource redistribution would also involve investing in infrastructure and economic development in underdeveloped regions. By building roads, schools, hospitals, and other critical infrastructure, we can create the conditions necessary for economic growth and development. This investment would not only improve the quality of life for people in these regions but also contribute to global prosperity by creating new markets and opportunities for trade.

The goal of global taxation and resource redistribution is to create a world in which everyone has the opportunity to thrive, regardless of where they were born. By pooling our resources and sharing them equitably, we can build a society that is fairer, more just, and more prosperous for all. The implementation of a global tax system may seem like a radical idea, but it is a necessary step toward achieving true global unity and addressing the challenges that threaten our collective future. Global taxation would ensure that every person, irrespective of their geographic location or economic background, benefits from the wealth generated worldwide. It would remove barriers that keep many people trapped in cycles of poverty and provide the necessary funding to address global issues such as climate change, pandemics, and food insecurity. By creating a system in which resources are allocated based on need rather than nationality or economic status, we can finally start to bridge the deep inequalities that have plagued humanity for centuries.

Moreover, global taxation would foster a sense of

collective responsibility, reminding us that we are all part of one interconnected human community. It would promote a culture of cooperation rather than competition, where countries and individuals work together to solve common problems. This shift in mindset is crucial if we are to overcome the divisions that have held us back for so long. By ensuring that everyone has access to basic necessities and opportunities, global taxation would not only reduce suffering but also unlock human potential on an unprecedented scale. Imagine a world where every child, regardless of where they are born, has access to quality education, where no one has to go without healthcare, and where poverty is no longer a barrier to achieving one's dreams. These are not just lofty ideals; they are attainable goals that can be realized through a well-implemented system of global taxation and resource redistribution.

The benefits of such a system would extend beyond economic stability and fairness. By addressing the root causes of inequality and creating an environment in which all people can thrive, we would also be laying the groundwork for a more peaceful world. Many of the conflicts that have scarred our history are rooted in competition for resources and opportunities. By creating a fairer, more equitable system, we can reduce these tensions and foster a spirit of solidarity and shared purpose. This transformation would allow humanity to move beyond the destructive patterns of the past and build a future defined by collaboration, innovation, and collective progress.

Global challenges require global solutions, and global taxation is one of the most powerful tools we have for addressing the inequalities that divide us. By redistributing wealth and resources, we can ensure that everyone has access to the opportunities they need to succeed. This is not just a moral imperative—it is also in our collective interest. A more equitable world is a more stable world, and by lifting up those who have been left behind, we can create a future of shared prosperity, peace, and cooperation.

In the next chapter, we will explore how global governance can provide the framework necessary to implement these solutions, ensuring that our shared resources are used wisely and that the interests of all people are represented. By creating a system of governance that transcends national borders, we can take another crucial step toward building a united world that works for everyone.

CHAPTER 6: GLOBAL GOVERNANCE AND THE CULTURE OF HUMAN IDENTITY

As we envision a future shaped by global unity, the establishment of global governance becomes a crucial step in transcending national boundaries and identities. In this new world order, we are no longer citizens of individual nations but rather global citizens, united by a common purpose and shared identity. The concept of global governance is not merely about managing resources or solving international problems; it is about fostering a collective consciousness and redefining what it means to belong. This chapter will explore how global governance can help facilitate the transition from fragmented national identities to a unified human identity, and how this transformation can pave the way for a more equitable, just, and sustainable world.

In the world we envision, national boundaries are no longer relevant. The traditional concept of nation-states—each with its own government, interests, and identity—has been replaced by a unified global system that serves the needs of all humanity. With the establishment of global governance, national borders have dissolved, allowing people the freedom to move, live, and work anywhere on the planet. This newfound freedom of movement eliminates the disparities created by artificial borders, allowing people to access opportunities regardless of their birthplace.

Global governance provides a framework for managing the planet's resources, addressing global challenges, and ensuring that all individuals have the opportunity to thrive. It serves as a guiding force to ensure that decisions are made in the best interest of humanity as a whole rather than catering to the short-term interests of individual nations. By eliminating borders, we can focus on what truly matters—creating a fair, just, and sustainable society for everyone. The end of national boundaries also removes the cause of countless conflicts throughout history, many of which have been fuelled by territorial disputes and the pursuit of national interests. Under global governance, these conflicts become a relic of the past, replaced by a commitment to cooperation and shared prosperity.

With the dissolution of national borders and the rise of global governance, a new culture of human identity emerges. This culture is not tied to any particular region, ethnicity, or religion but is based on the shared values and experiences of all human beings. It emphasizes our common humanity, celebrating what unites us rather than what divides us. The culture of human identity recognizes that while our histories and backgrounds may differ, our fundamental needs and aspirations are the same —we all desire safety, prosperity, connection, and purpose.

To fully embrace a culture of human identity, it is necessary to let go of the cultural divisions that have long separated us. The labels of nationality, ethnicity, and religion have often been used to divide people, creating an "us versus them" mentality that has fuelled conflict, prejudice, and misunderstanding. These divisions have often led to exclusion, discrimination, and even violence, making it difficult for people to see beyond their immediate affiliations and recognize the common humanity that unites us all. In a world governed by a global system, these labels become irrelevant, replaced by the understanding that we are all members of the same human family. This new perspective allows us to redefine our identity beyond artificial and superficial markers, fostering an environment where everyone is valued equally, and no one is marginalized based on arbitrary characteristics. By embracing a global culture, we can begin to dismantle the barriers that have kept us apart, building a society where cooperation and empathy take precedence over division and mistrust.

The culture of human identity also emphasizes the importance of collective well-being. In the past, people have often prioritized the interests of their own country or community, sometimes at the expense of others. This narrow focus has created a fragmented world where competition has taken precedence over collaboration, and where the success of one group often comes at the detriment of another. Under global governance, our focus shifts to what benefits humanity as a whole, recognizing that our fates are intertwined, and that the well-being of any one individual or community is directly linked to the well-being of all. This cultural shift is essential for addressing the challenges that threaten our shared future, such as climate change, resource scarcity, and global inequality. By redefining our sense of identity to include all people, we create a foundation for genuine cooperation, where our shared commitment to solving the problems that affect us all becomes a driving force for progress. This redefined identity encourages us to view every challenge as a shared responsibility, fostering a spirit of unity and purpose that transcends borders and brings us closer together as one global family.

The establishment of global governance would involve the creation of institutions that represent the interests of all people, regardless of their background or place of origin. These institutions would be responsible for making decisions on issues that impact humanity as a whole, such as environmental protection, resource management, and global health. The Global Council, for example, would be a representative body tasked with ensuring that the voices of all regions are heard and that policies are created with the well-being of every individual in mind.

The goal of global governance is to create a system in which power is distributed fairly, with decisions made based on the principles of equity, justice, and sustainability. Unlike the current system, where powerful nations often dominate international decision-making, global governance would ensure that every person has a voice and that the interests of all people are considered. This inclusive approach to governance is essential for building a world where everyone has the opportunity to thrive, free from the constraints of inequality and discrimination.

The Global Revenue Authority, as discussed in the previous chapter, would serve as a key component of global governance, collecting and redistributing resources to ensure that every individual has access to the basic necessities of life. This system of resource redistribution would help eliminate the disparities that currently exist between nations, ensuring that all people have access to education, healthcare, and economic opportunities. By creating a system that prioritizes the well-being of all people, we can build a society that is more just, equitable, and resilient.

Under global governance, every individual becomes a global citizen, with rights and responsibilities that extend beyond the borders of any one country. As global citizens, we are no longer tied to the narrow interests of a single nation but are instead committed to the well-being of all humanity. This shift in identity empowers individuals to take an active role in shaping the future of the world, knowing that their actions have a direct impact on the collective good.

Global citizenship also involves a commitment to sustainable living and social responsibility. As citizens of the world, we must be mindful of the impact our actions have on the planet and on other people. This means adopting practices that promote environmental sustainability, supporting policies that reduce inequality, and working together to create a society that benefits everyone. By embracing our role as global citizens, we can create a culture of care and responsibility that transcends borders and fosters a sense of unity and purpose.

The concept of global citizenship is also about empowerment. In a world governed by a global system, individuals have the power to contribute to meaningful change on a global scale. Whether through participating in decision-making processes, advocating for social justice, or supporting initiatives that promote sustainability, global citizens are empowered to play an active role in shaping the future. This sense of empowerment is crucial for building a world where everyone feels that they have a stake in the future and that their voice matters.

The transition to global governance and the adoption of a human identity culture is not without its challenges. Many people may struggle to let go of the cultural and national identities that have shaped their lives. However, the benefits of embracing a unified global identity far outweigh the difficulties of change. By adopting a culture of human identity, we can build a world that is more peaceful, equitable, and sustainable—a world where every individual has the opportunity to thrive.

The path forward requires a collective commitment to reimagining governance, reshaping our identities, and redefining our values. It requires us to move beyond the divisions of the past and embrace a future where we are all part of a single, interconnected human family. By working together to establish global governance, we can create a system that reflects our shared values and aspirations, ensuring that the interests of all people are represented and that the challenges we face are addressed collectively.

The journey toward global governance and the culture of human identity is a bold one, but it is also a necessary step toward building a better future for all of humanity. By transcending the divisions of the past and embracing our common humanity, we can create a world that is defined not by conflict and competition, but by cooperation, empathy, and shared purpose. In the next chapter, we will explore the role of education and awareness in fostering this cultural shift, examining how we can educate future generations to think beyond borders and embrace their role as global citizens in an interconnected world.

CHAPTER 7: EDUCATION AND AWARENESS: FOSTERING GLOBAL CITIZENSHIP

The journey toward a united world built on the foundation of global governance and a human identity culture requires a profound transformation in the way we think, act, and relate to each other. This transformation begins with education and awareness—the tools through which we can nurture the values, skills, and knowledge needed to become true global citizens. Education is not merely about gaining academic knowledge; it is about understanding our place in the world, the responsibilities that come with it, and the impact of our actions on the global community. This chapter explores the role of education in fostering global citizenship, breaking down cultural barriers, and encouraging the adoption of a unified human identity.

Education is the cornerstone of progress. It has the power to shape our values, challenge our biases, and expand our perspectives. In the context of global citizenship, education must move beyond the traditional focus on national history, culture, and achievements, and instead embrace a broader view of humanity as a whole. By teaching future generations about the interconnectedness of the world, we can help them understand that the challenges we face—such as climate change, inequality, and global health crises—are not confined to any one country or region. They are global problems that require global solutions, and their resolution depends on cooperation, empathy, and a sense of shared responsibility.

A curriculum designed to foster global consciousness would include subjects like global history, sustainable development, human rights, and the importance of shared human identity. Students would learn about the interdependence of nations, the impact of historical injustices, and the importance of sustainability for the future of the planet. By exposing young people to a diverse range of perspectives, we can help them move beyond the limitations of national or cultural identity and encourage them to see themselves as part of a broader human family. This approach to education would also emphasize critical thinking, encouraging students to question assumptions, recognize biases, and understand the complex relationships between local actions and global outcomes.

One of the greatest obstacles to achieving global unity is the existence of cultural barriers—those deep-rooted beliefs, practices, and traditions that separate us from one another. While culture has historically been a source of identity and belonging, it has also been a source of division, prejudice, and conflict. The goal of education in fostering global citizenship is to help people understand that while our backgrounds may differ, our fundamental human needs and aspirations are the same, and that these needs are best served by transcending cultural divisions.

Through education, we can promote the idea that cultural divisions are ultimately barriers to progress and unity. By teaching the value of a human identity that transcends national and cultural affiliations, we can help individuals see that clinging to old cultural markers only perpetuates separation, mistrust, and conflict. Education should encourage individuals to abandon outdated cultural constructs and instead embrace the identity of being human above all else. By doing so, we can dismantle the barriers that have kept us apart, building a society where cooperation, shared purpose, and mutual understanding take precedence over division and mistrust.

To fully break down cultural barriers, education must go beyond simply highlighting the commonalities between people—it must actively challenge the assumptions and biases that reinforce cultural divisions. This means creating learning environments that encourage open dialogue, critical examination of cultural norms, and a willingness to let go of practices that do not serve the greater good of humanity. It also involves emphasizing the importance of empathy not in the context of preserving cultural diversity, but in the context of understanding the shared human experience and recognizing that our collective well-being is more important than individual cultural identities.

Programs like global collaboration projects, international learning initiatives, and unified educational frameworks can play a significant role in breaking down cultural barriers and building a sense of solidarity among young people from different parts of the world. By creating opportunities for direct engagement and shared experiences, these programs help individuals realize that despite our differences, we are all part of the same global community. This realization is essential for fostering the sense of unity and collective purpose that is at the heart of global governance. These initiatives must focus on creating a new culture—one that is not rooted in past traditions but is instead centred on our shared goals, values, and aspirations as human beings.

In addition, the role of educators is crucial in guiding students to adopt a human identity over traditional cultural labels. Teachers must be equipped to facilitate discussions that question the validity and relevance of cultural divisions, helping students to see how these divisions have historically held humanity back from achieving true progress. By encouraging young people to see themselves as part of a unified human family, educators can inspire a new generation to work towards a future that is defined not by where we come from, but by what we can achieve together. This transformation in mindset is key to overcoming the barriers that have kept us divided and building a society that prioritizes collaboration, equity, and a shared vision for the future.

Beyond formal education, awareness campaigns play a critical role in fostering global citizenship. Awareness initiatives can be used to educate people about the pressing challenges facing humanity, such as climate change, poverty, and inequality, and inspire them to take action. These campaigns can leverage various platforms—including social media, public events, and community organizations—to reach diverse audiences and encourage widespread participation in efforts to address global issues.

For example, campaigns that highlight the effects

of climate change on vulnerable populations can help people understand that the consequences of environmental degradation are not just abstract concepts; they have real and immediate impacts on people's lives. By creating a personal connection to these issues, awareness campaigns can inspire individuals to adopt more sustainable practices, support policies that promote environmental protection, and advocate for systemic change. Similarly, campaigns focused on human rights can help people recognize the importance of equity and justice, encouraging them to abandon divisive cultural identities and instead embrace a collective human identity.

Awareness campaigns are also vital in promoting the concept of global citizenship. Many people still identify primarily with their nationality, ethnicity, or religion, and may find it difficult to let go of these identities in favour of a broader human identity. By highlighting the benefits of global governance—such as increased peace, prosperity, and opportunity—awareness initiatives can help individuals see that embracing a global identity is about moving beyond the limitations of cultural heritage to achieve a deeper connection to the entire human family. These campaigns can help shift mindsets, encouraging people to see themselves as citizens of the world with a responsibility to contribute to the well-being of all.

Education is also a powerful tool for empowerment.

By providing individuals with the knowledge, skills, and resources they need to succeed, we can create a more equitable world where everyone has the opportunity to thrive. This is particularly important for marginalized communities, who have often been excluded from educational opportunities and denied the chance to participate fully in society. By investing in education for all, we can help lift people out of poverty, reduce inequality, and create a more just and inclusive world.

In the context of global citizenship, education must also empower individuals to take action. It is not enough to understand the challenges we face; we must also be equipped to address them. This means providing people with the skills they need to advocate for change, whether at the local, national, or global level. It also means creating opportunities for individuals to get involved in initiatives that promote sustainability, social justice, and global cooperation. By empowering people to take action, we can create a culture of active global citizenship, where everyone feels that they have a role to play in building a better future.

Technology plays an increasingly important role in education and awareness, particularly in the context of fostering global citizenship. Digital platforms can connect people from different parts of the world, providing opportunities for learning, collaboration, and dialogue that were previously unimaginable. Online courses, virtual exchange programs, and global discussion forums can help individuals gain a deeper understanding of global issues and develop a sense of connection to people in other countries.

Technology also allows for the rapid dissemination of information, making it easier to raise awareness about global challenges and mobilize people to take action. Social media platforms, for example, have been used to organize movements, share stories, and create a sense of solidarity among people from different backgrounds. By harnessing the power of technology, we can create a more informed and engaged global citizenry, capable of contributing to meaningful change on a global scale. Technology also serves as a tool to break down cultural divisions, as it exposes individuals to diverse perspectives and encourages them to see the value in embracing a unified human identity over maintaining outdated cultural affiliations.

The path toward global governance and a human identity culture is one that requires continuous learning, growth, and adaptation. Education and awareness are the cornerstones of this journey, providing the knowledge, skills, and values needed to build a united world. By fostering a sense of global citizenship in future generations, we can create a culture of cooperation and shared responsibility —one that transcends borders and embraces our common humanity.

The journey will not be without its challenges. Many people may resist the idea of letting go of the cultural and national identities that have defined them for so long. However, by investing in education and promoting awareness, we can help individuals see the value of a unified human identity and inspire them to become active participants in shaping a better future for all. The power of education lies not only in what we learn but also in how we apply that knowledge to create

CHAPTER 8: TECHNOLOGY AND INNOVATION: BUILDING A FUTURE FOR ALL

In the journey toward a unified world based on global governance and a human identity culture, technology and innovation serve as key enablers. They offer tools that can help overcome many of the challenges we face today and create new opportunities for growth, equality, and sustainability. To achieve the vision of a world that thrives as one interconnected community, we must harness the transformative potential of technology and ensure that its benefits are accessible to everyone. This chapter explores how technological advancements can support global governance, enhance quality of life, and foster a shared future for all.

Technology has the power to connect people in ways that were once unimaginable. Through the internet and digital platforms, individuals across the globe can communicate, share experiences, and work together toward common goals. This connectivity breaks down physical and psychological barriers, enabling people to transcend geographic distances and national identities to see themselves as part of a broader human family.

Social media, online learning platforms, and collaborative tools provide opportunities for individuals to interact and learn from one another, promoting understanding and cooperation. For instance, online forums and discussion groups give people the chance to engage with perspectives from different backgrounds, broadening their understanding of global issues. These platforms also serve as tools for advocacy and activism, helping to amplify voices that might otherwise go unheard. In this way, technology serves as both a bridge and a megaphone, empowering individuals to participate in the creation of a more just and equitable world.

Artificial intelligence (AI), virtual reality (VR), and augmented reality (AR) are also contributing to the development of global consciousness by offering immersive experiences that allow people to walk in someone else's shoes, understand different ways of life, and cultivate empathy for others. These technologies help people see beyond their own experiences, facilitating a deeper understanding of what it means to be part of the global community. By making the invisible visible, technology plays a critical role in fostering a culture of empathy, cooperation, and shared purpose.

While technology has the potential to unify, it also has the potential to create divides if not managed equitably. Digital inequality—the gap between those who have access to technology and those who do not—remains a significant challenge in realizing a united world. To truly benefit from technology's unifying power, it is essential that access to technological tools and the internet is available to everyone, regardless of their location or socioeconomic status.

To bridge this gap, global governance must prioritize digital inclusivity. This means investing in the infrastructure needed to provide reliable internet access to all communities, especially those that have been historically underserved. It also means ensuring that people have the skills and education they need to use technology effectively. Digital literacy programs, community technology centres, and public-private partnerships can all play a role in closing the digital divide and making sure that no one is left behind as the world moves toward greater technological integration.

Global institutes must be created that are responsible for ensuring that technology is made available to all global citizens. These institutes would oversee not only the distribution of technological resources but also the development of educational programs to ensure everyone has the skills necessary to utilize these tools effectively. Tax resources would be invested to balance out inequality and support the technological infrastructure required to bridge the digital divide. Such investments would include building internet infrastructure in underserved areas, subsidizing technology access for all citizens, and supporting initiatives that foster digital literacy and innovation.

In the end, providing the technological tools to all citizens will benefit humanity as a whole. We could find the next Albert Einstein or Elon Musk whose potential would never have been uncovered without the proper investment. By creating an environment where everyone has equal access to technology, we can unlock untapped potential and empower individuals to contribute to the global community in meaningful ways. Imagine the breakthroughs in science, medicine, and sustainability that could emerge if every individual, regardless of their background, had the opportunity to explore, innovate, and solve the challenges facing humanity. This collective advancement would not only enrich individual lives but also drive progress and prosperity for the entire human race.

Sustainability is another critical area where

technology and innovation can support the vision of a united world. The challenges we face—such as climate change, resource depletion, and environmental degradation—require coordinated efforts and innovative solutions that prioritize the health of the planet and the well-being of all people. Technology offers powerful tools that can help us address these challenges and create a more sustainable future.

Renewable energy technologies, such as solar, wind, and hydropower, are examples of innovations that can help reduce our reliance on fossil fuels and mitigate the impacts of climate change. Advances in energy storage and smart grids are also making it possible to manage energy more efficiently and ensure that renewable energy sources are available when and where they are needed. By investing in these technologies and making them accessible to all, global governance can promote a more sustainable energy future that benefits everyone.

In addition to energy, technology can also support sustainable practices in agriculture, waste management, and water conservation. For example, precision agriculture uses sensors, drones, and data analytics to optimize farming practices, reducing waste and improving crop yields. Circular economy technologies, such as recycling innovations and waste-to-energy systems, can help minimize environmental impact by reusing materials and reducing the amount of waste that ends up in landfills. These technological solutions, when implemented globally, can help ensure that the planet's resources are managed in a way that is fair and sustainable for all.

Healthcare is another area where technology and innovation can have a transformative impact. The COVID-19 pandemic demonstrated both the power of technology to respond to global health crises and the gaps that still need to be addressed. By leveraging technology, we can create a global healthcare system that is more resilient, accessible, and effective.

Telemedicine and digital health platforms have already shown their potential to extend healthcare services to remote and underserved communities. By making medical expertise available online, these technologies can help ensure that everyone, regardless of their location, has access to quality healthcare. Artificial intelligence is also being used to improve diagnostics, personalize treatment plans, and predict disease outbreaks, allowing for a more proactive approach to healthcare.

To create a world where health and well-being are truly universal, global governance must invest in these innovations and ensure that they are accessible to all. This means not only funding research and development but also creating policies that make healthcare technologies affordable and widely available. It also means addressing the ethical considerations that come with new technologies, such as data privacy and the equitable distribution of medical resources. By doing so, we can create a healthcare system that serves the needs of the entire human family.

Technology and innovation have the power to bring us closer to the vision of a united world where everyone can thrive. However, this future will not happen on its own—it requires intentional action, investment, and collaboration from all sectors of society, including governments, private companies, and individuals. Global governance must take the lead in ensuring that technological advancements are used to benefit all of humanity, rather than exacerbating existing inequalities or creating new ones. This leadership requires proactive policies, strategic partnerships, and a commitment to equitable access to technology on a global scale. To truly harness the potential of technology for good, we need a comprehensive framework that guides how technology is developed, distributed, and used to create a more inclusive and prosperous world.

By focusing on digital inclusivity, sustainable development, and universal access to healthcare, we can create a world where technology serves as a tool for empowerment, equality, and progress. This vision requires a shift in mindset—from seeing technology as a means of individual gain to viewing it as a collective resource that can help solve the challenges we face together. It also demands that we rethink how technological advancements are shared, ensuring that developing nations and marginalized communities are not left behind. Achieving this vision will involve fostering public-private partnerships that prioritize social impact over profit and implementing policies that promote open access to technological innovations. It also requires us to move beyond national interests and embrace a human identity culture that prioritizes the well-being of all people, regardless of where they are from. Only by uniting our efforts can we ensure that technology fulfils its potential as a force for good in the world, fostering not only innovation but also genuine, lasting equity and harmony across all societies.

In the next chapter, we will explore how economic systems must evolve to support a united world under global governance. We will discuss the importance of a minimum living wage for all working-age citizens, the role of universal taxation, and the ways in which economic policies can be reimagined to promote equality, stability, and shared prosperity for all.

CHAPTER 9: EVOLVING ECONOMIC SYSTEMS: BUILDING A FOUNDATION FOR EQUALITY AND STABILITY

As we move toward a world defined by global governance and a shared human identity, our economic systems must evolve to support this new reality. Traditional economic models have often prioritized individual gain, competition, and national interests, leading to significant inequalities and creating barriers to global unity. To foster a sustainable, equitable, and prosperous future for all, we need to reimagine economic systems in a way that supports not only economic growth but also fairness, stability, and the well-being of every global citizen. This chapter explores how economic systems can be transformed to support the goals of global governance, with a focus on minimum living wages, universal taxation, and collective prosperity.

One of the most essential elements of an equitable economic system is the establishment of a minimum living wage for every working-age citizen in the world. This wage would be guaranteed regardless of whether an individual is currently employed or not, providing stability for those between jobs, pursuing education, or contributing to society in non-traditional ways. A minimum living wage is a recognition of the inherent value of every human being and their right to a dignified life.

A minimum living wage would serve multiple purposes. First, it would address the issue of economic inequality by providing financial security to those who are most vulnerable. This would help reduce poverty and allow individuals to focus on opportunities for growth and development rather than merely surviving. Second, it would stimulate the global economy by increasing consumer spending, as more people would have the means to participate in the market. This boost in economic activity would benefit businesses and communities, ultimately fostering global prosperity.

The concept of a minimum living wage also supports the idea of human identity by reinforcing the belief that every person, regardless of their background or circumstances, deserves a fair opportunity to thrive. By providing a safety net that ensures basic needs are met, we can create a foundation for greater social cohesion and unity, enabling people to contribute to society in ways that align with their skills, passions, and aspirations. This approach prioritizes collective well-being over individual wealth accumulation and shifts the focus from economic survival to personal and societal growth.

In a world governed by a unified global authority, economic policies must be restructured to align with the principles of fairness, equality, and shared responsibility. One of the most significant changes required is the implementation of a universal taxation system. Rather than paying taxes to local or federal governments, individuals and corporations would contribute to a global fund designed to support initiatives that benefit all of humanity. Essentially, all national and local taxes would be eliminated and replaced by a system of global taxation that ensures resources are distributed in a way that promotes collective prosperity.

A universal taxation system would have several key benefits. It would provide the necessary funding for global initiatives such as healthcare, education, infrastructure development, and climate action. By pooling resources at a global level, we could address issues that no single nation can tackle alone, such as pandemics, poverty, and environmental degradation. Additionally, universal taxation would help to reduce tax avoidance and wealth inequality by creating a system that ensures everyone contributes their fair share, regardless of where they are located or how much wealth they possess.

This approach would also foster a sense of global citizenship by emphasizing the idea that we are all part of a single human community with shared responsibilities. By eliminating the competition between nations for tax revenue and investment, we can create an environment where decisions are made based on what is best for humanity as a whole rather than individual national interests. A universal taxation system is an essential component of a fair and just economic model that supports the goals of global governance and a united human identity.

To build a world where everyone can thrive, we must go beyond the concept of a minimum living wage and universal taxation and reimagine our economic policies in a way that promotes shared prosperity. This means shifting from an economic system that prioritizes competition and profit maximization at all costs to one that values cooperation, sustainability, and equity. However, it is important to emphasize that businesses and companies will still play a crucial role in this new system. We want companies to succeed, make profits, and continue to employ people, thereby contributing to the global economy through taxation. The key is to strike a balance between maximizing profit and ensuring global responsibility, creating a system where businesses can thrive while also contributing to the collective well-being of humanity.

Economic policies should be designed to ensure that the benefits of growth are distributed fairly, that opportunities are available to all, and that no one is left behind. This involves creating an environment where businesses can operate successfully while adhering to ethical practices that support the common good. We still want businesses to innovate, grow, and generate wealth, but this must be done in a way that aligns with the broader goals of global unity and well-being.

Another key element of shared prosperity is investment in education and skills development. In a rapidly changing world, where technology and innovation are driving economic transformation, it is essential that everyone has access to the education and training they need to succeed. Global governance must prioritize investment in education, ensuring that all people, regardless of their background, have the opportunity to develop the skills they need to participate in the global economy. This includes not only traditional education but also lifelong learning opportunities that enable individuals to adapt to changing circumstances and continue to grow throughout their lives.

Sustainable development must also be at the core of our economic policies. By investing in technologies and practices that promote environmental sustainability, we can create an economy that not only supports human well-being but also protects the planet for future generations. This includes transitioning to renewable energy, promoting circular economies that reduce waste, and encouraging responsible consumption and production practices. A sustainable economy is one that balances the needs of people, the planet, and prosperity, ensuring that we can continue to thrive as a global community for generations to come.

The evolution of our economic systems is crucial to building a world where everyone can thrive. By establishing a minimum living wage, implementing universal taxation, and reimagining economic policies to promote shared prosperity, we can create a foundation for equality, stability, and progress. These changes are not just about improving the quality of life for individuals—they are about fostering a sense of global citizenship, where everyone feels a sense of responsibility for the well-being of others and the future of our planet.

In a world governed by global governance, economic systems must serve the collective good rather than individual interests. By embracing the principles of fairness, equity, and sustainability, we can create an economy that supports the vision of a united human family—a world where everyone has the opportunity to thrive, contribute, and achieve their fullest potential. The transformation of our economic systems is not an easy task, but it is a necessary one if we are to build a future defined by peace, prosperity, and unity.

In the next chapter, we will explore how political systems must evolve to support the goals of global governance. We will discuss the importance of a unified global government, the role of democratic participation, and the ways in which political structures can be reimagined to ensure that the voices of all people are heard and respected in the decision-making process.

CHAPTER 10: EVOLVING POLITICAL SYSTEMS: THE PATH TO GLOBAL GOVERNANCE

With the transformation of economic systems to promote equality, stability, and collective well-being, it is equally important to rethink and evolve our political systems to support the vision of global governance. To achieve a world defined by peace, prosperity, and unity, we must adopt a political framework that transcends national borders and individual interests, ensuring that all people have a voice in the decisions that affect their lives. This chapter will explore how political systems must evolve to align with the goals of global governance, emphasizing the importance of a unified global government, democratic participation, and inclusive decision-making processes.

To effectively address the complex challenges facing humanity today, from climate change to global pandemics, it is essential to establish a unified global government. The problems we face are not confined by national borders, and as such, solutions must be developed and implemented on a global scale. A unified global government would provide the leadership and coordination necessary to tackle these challenges head-on, ensuring that decisions are made in the best interests of all people rather than individual nations.

A unified global government would also eliminate the conflicts and competition that have historically arisen from competing national interests. By shifting our focus from national sovereignty to collective responsibility, we can create an environment where cooperation becomes the norm and where the well-being of humanity takes precedence over political power struggles. This transition would enable us to pool our resources, expertise, and innovations to build a sustainable and equitable world for all.

It is important to recognize that a unified global government does not mean the loss of local representation or governance. Instead, it represents a shift in how we address issues that impact the entire planet. Global borders will be redrawn for administrative purposes only, creating administrative zones that allow for localized governance. Each administrative zone will have a representative body responsible for managing day-to-day matters unique to their communities, while the global government would address issues of collective importance, such as environmental protection, global health, and security. This balance would allow for effective governance at every level, ensuring that both local and global needs are met. Furthermore, a unified global government would provide a platform for administrative zones to work collaboratively, sharing resources and knowledge to overcome common challenges and achieve shared objectives.

A successful global government must be built on the foundation of democratic participation. Every individual, regardless of their background or nationality, must have a say in the decisions that shape their lives and the future of humanity. To ensure that the voices of all people are heard, and respected, political systems must evolve to facilitate inclusive and equitable participation on a global scale.

In this new system, people will vote in the administrative zone where they currently reside, rather than the country in which they were born. This approach emphasizes the concept of a borderless world, where individuals are empowered to participate in the governance of their communities based on their present context and contributions. Each administrative zone will have a representative body that is elected by the people living in that area. These representative bodies will then elect a representative to sit on the global council, ensuring that every administrative zone has a voice in the global decision-making process.

To achieve this, we need to create mechanisms that allow individuals to engage in decision-making processes at all levels of governance. This could include the establishment of global voting platforms, where citizens can vote on major global initiatives, as well as the formation of representative bodies that ensure the diverse perspectives of all communities are considered. By making participation accessible and inclusive, we can create a global government that truly represents the will of the people and works in the best interests of humanity.

In addition to voting, it is essential to foster a culture of civic engagement and political awareness. Education plays a crucial role in this regard, as it helps individuals understand the importance of their participation and equips them with the knowledge and skills needed to contribute effectively to the political process. By investing in education and creating opportunities for civic engagement, we can empower people to take an active role in shaping the future of our global society. Civic engagement can take many forms, including community organizing, advocacy for social causes, and participation in public forums where critical issues are discussed. Encouraging such engagement at both local and global levels will ensure that the principles of democracy are upheld, and that the governance structures are responsive to the needs and aspirations of all citizens.

For global governance to be effective and just, it is crucial that decision-making processes are inclusive and fair. This means that all people, regardless of their nationality, ethnicity, or socioeconomic status, must have an equal opportunity to influence the policies and actions of the global government. Historically, marginalized communities have often been excluded from political processes, resulting in decisions that do not reflect their needs or interests. To build a truly equitable global society, we must ensure that these voices are not only heard but also prioritized.

One way to achieve this is by establishing representative bodies that reflect the diversity of humanity within each administrative zone. These bodies would be responsible for ensuring that the perspectives of all communities are taken into account when making decisions that impact the global population. In addition, decision-making processes must be transparent and accountable, with mechanisms in place to prevent corruption and ensure that the global government operates in the best interests of all people. Transparency can be enhanced through open forums, regular reporting, and the use of technology to make information accessible to all. Citizens should have the right to hold their representatives accountable through mechanisms like public reviews, recall procedures, and independent oversight bodies.

Another important aspect of inclusive decision-making is the recognition and protection of individual rights. A global government must be committed to upholding the fundamental rights of every person, including the right to freedom of expression, freedom of assembly, and freedom from discrimination. By safeguarding these rights, we can create an environment where all people feel empowered to participate in the political process and contribute to the collective well-being of humanity. It is essential that these rights are protected by enforceable international laws, ensuring that violations are met with appropriate consequences and that every individual feels secure in their ability to express themselves and participate in society.

The evolution of political systems to support global governance will require a significant shift in mindset, as well as the establishment of new institutions and frameworks that prioritize cooperation over competition. Building trust among administrative zones, and individuals is a crucial step in this process. For many, the idea of a unified global government may seem daunting or even threatening, as it challenges the traditional notions of national sovereignty and identity. However, by focusing on our shared challenges and common goals, we can begin to build a sense of global solidarity that transcends borders and unites us as one human family.

International cooperation will be key to the success of global governance. Administrative zones must be willing to set aside their individual interests and work together for the greater good of humanity. This will require the development of binding agreements and shared frameworks that ensure all regions are held accountable for their actions and contribute to the collective effort. By fostering a spirit of collaboration and mutual respect, we can create a political system that supports the well-being of all people and the sustainability of our planet. Building trust will also involve recognizing past injustices and working towards reconciliation. By addressing historical grievances and committing to fairness and equality, we can foster a sense of unity and build a political culture rooted in trust and cooperation.

The evolution of our political systems is essential to achieving the vision of a united, prosperous, and peaceful world. By establishing a unified global government, ensuring democratic participation, and creating inclusive and fair decision-making processes, we can build a political framework that serves the interests of all humanity. This transformation is not without its challenges, but it is a necessary step if we are to address the complex issues facing our world today and create a future where everyone can thrive.

As we move forward, it is important to remember that global governance is not about erasing local cultures or identities. Instead, it is about embracing our shared human identity and working together to solve the problems that affect us all. By creating a political system that prioritizes cooperation, inclusivity, and collective well-being, we can build a world where everyone has the opportunity to contribute, succeed, and live a dignified life. This vision requires us to think beyond our immediate surroundings and recognize the interconnectedness of all people. By fostering empathy, mutual respect, and a commitment to the common good, we can create a political system that ensures a brighter and more equitable future for all.

In the next chapter, we will explore how cultural transformation is crucial to supporting the goals of global governance and a shared human identity. We will discuss the importance of letting go of divisive cultural identities and embracing a new culture of unity, empathy, and collective progress.

CHAPTER 11: CULTURAL TRANSFORMATION: EMBRACING A SHARED HUMAN IDENTITY

With the establishment of global governance and the reimagining of our economic and political systems, the next crucial step in building a unified world is to transform our cultural understanding. Cultural transformation is about letting go of the divisive aspects of our past and embracing a new, shared identity that unites us all as members of the human race. This chapter will explore the importance of cultural transformation, the challenges it presents, and how we can work collectively to replace old cultural divisions with a new sense of unity, empathy, and collective progress.

Throughout history, cultural identities have provided people with a sense of belonging, tradition, and continuity. These identities have often been defined by ethnicity, nationality, religion, and other markers that separate individuals into distinct groups. However, these same identities have also been the root of much of humanity's division, conflict, and suffering. To achieve true global unity, we must be willing to let go of these divisive cultural markers and instead adopt an identity based on our common humanity.

Letting go of cultural identity can be incredibly challenging. It often feels like a betrayal of one's heritage, ancestors, and community. People naturally value the traditions and beliefs that have been passed down through generations, and abandoning these can create a sense of loss and disorientation. It is essential to recognize that this process of cultural transformation will not happen overnight and will require patience, empathy, and understanding. We must provide support to those who struggle with this transition, helping them see the value in embracing a shared human identity that promotes peace, equality, and cooperation.

The concept of a shared human identity is built on the idea that we are all part of one global family, with shared goals and challenges that transcend our individual backgrounds. By letting go of divisive cultural identities, we can eliminate the barriers that have kept us from working together effectively as a species. This transformation allows us to focus on what truly matters: ensuring the well-being of all people, protecting the environment, and creating a future where everyone can thrive.

A shared human identity fosters a sense of empathy and solidarity. When we see ourselves not as members of separate cultural groups but as human beings with common experiences and aspirations, we are more likely to act with compassion and care for others. This shift in perspective can lead to a reduction in prejudice, discrimination, and conflict, paving the way for a more harmonious and equitable world.

In addition, a shared human identity can drive innovation and progress. When we move beyond the limitations imposed by cultural divisions, we open ourselves up to new ideas, perspectives, and ways of thinking. Collaboration becomes easier when people are not constrained by cultural biases, and this can lead to breakthroughs in science, technology, and social development that benefit all of humanity. By working together as one, we can achieve things that would be impossible if we remained divided.

Education is a powerful tool for driving cultural transformation and helping people embrace a shared human identity. By teaching future generations about the value of unity, cooperation, and empathy, we can create a foundation for a more inclusive and interconnected world. Schools, universities, and community programs should focus on fostering a sense of global citizenship, helping individuals understand that their well-being is tied to the well-being of others around the world.

Educational initiatives should emphasize the importance of critical thinking and open-mindedness, encouraging people to question cultural norms that promote division and instead adopt values that support collective progress. By providing opportunities for individuals to engage with people from different backgrounds, we can help break down the barriers that have traditionally separated us and build a culture of mutual respect and understanding.

Furthermore, media and communication play a significant role in shaping cultural attitudes. By promoting stories, narratives, and representations that highlight our shared humanity, we can begin to shift public perception away from the idea of cultural differences as a source of conflict. Instead, we can focus on the values and aspirations that unite us, helping people see that our similarities far outweigh our differences.

To achieve cultural transformation, we must actively work to build a new culture that prioritizes unity and collective progress. This means creating spaces and opportunities for people to come together, share experiences, and work towards common goals. Community initiatives, global events, and collaborative projects can help foster a sense of shared purpose and belonging, allowing individuals to feel connected to something greater than themselves.

One way to build a culture of unity is through global celebrations that emphasize our shared achievements and milestones. Instead of focusing on national holidays that celebrate individual countries, we can create new traditions that celebrate humanity's progress as a whole. These celebrations can serve as reminders of what we can accomplish when we work together and can help reinforce the idea that we are all part of the same global community.

Art and culture also have a significant role to play in this transformation. By encouraging artistic expressions that reflect our shared human experience, we can create a new cultural narrative that transcends borders and brings people together. Music, literature, visual arts, and other forms of creative expression can help convey the emotions, struggles, and triumphs that are universal to all people, fostering a deeper sense of connection and empathy.

The journey towards cultural transformation will not be easy, but it is a necessary step if we are to achieve the vision of a united and prosperous world. By letting go of the cultural identities that have divided us for so long, we can embrace a new identity that is based on our shared humanity and collective potential. This transformation will require effort at every level of society, from individuals and communities to governments and global institutions.

It is important to remember that embracing a shared human identity does not mean erasing our personal histories or the unique experiences that have shaped us. Instead, it means recognizing that our differences are less important than the common goals and values that unite us. By focusing on what we have in common, we can build a future where everyone has the opportunity to thrive, free from the divisions and conflicts that have held us back for so long.

As we move forward, we must remain committed to the principles of empathy, cooperation, and collective progress. By working together to transform our cultural understanding, we can create a world where every person is valued, every voice is heard, and every individual has the opportunity to contribute to the greater good. This is the vision of a shared human identity—a world where we are not defined by our differences but by our potential to achieve greatness together.

In the next chapter, we will explore the practical steps that individuals, communities, and governments can take to promote and support the cultural transformation needed for global unity. We will discuss specific actions that can help create a more inclusive world, from education and advocacy to policy changes and grassroots movements.

CHAPTER 12: PRACTICAL STEPS TOWARD CULTURAL TRANSFORMATION AND GLOBAL UNITY

Having explored the necessity of cultural transformation and the need to embrace a shared human identity, we now turn our focus to the practical steps that individuals, communities, and governments can take to make this vision a reality. Cultural transformation is not just a theoretical shift; it is a process that requires action, commitment, and concrete changes at every level of society. In this chapter, we will outline actionable strategies that can promote cultural transformation and pave the way toward global unity.

Individual Actions: Embracing Human Identity in Daily Life

The journey towards a shared human identity begins with the actions of individuals. Each person has the power to contribute to cultural transformation by making small but meaningful changes in their daily lives. Some practical steps include:

Think Globally, Act Locally: Recognize that your actions impact the broader world, and take steps to reduce harm while promoting positive change. Support causes that reflect global values, such as environmental sustainability, social justice, and human rights.

Challenge Cultural Biases: Question and reflect on the cultural biases and assumptions that you have internalized over time. Make a conscious effort to understand perspectives that differ from your own and embrace the concept of a shared human identity.

Cultivate Empathy: Practice empathy in your interactions with others by putting yourself in their shoes and considering their challenges. Empathy is a powerful tool for breaking down barriers and fostering unity.

Engage in Global Citizenship: Participate in global causes and initiatives. This could involve supporting international relief efforts, promoting environmental initiatives, or advocating for human rights. By taking part in efforts that benefit all of humanity, you actively promote global unity.

Community Initiatives: Building a Culture of Collaboration

Communities are at the core of cultural transformation. By fostering a sense of collaboration and mutual support, communities can help bridge the gaps that have historically divided us. Practical community-level initiatives include:

Organize Community Dialogues: Establish forums or discussion groups where people from different backgrounds can come together to share their experiences and perspectives. Such dialogues help break down stereotypes, foster mutual understanding, and build solidarity.

Create Global Celebrations: Develop events that celebrate our shared human achievements rather than emphasizing national or ethnic distinctions. These celebrations can serve as opportunities to bring people together in a spirit of unity.

Support Inclusive Education: Advocate for and support educational programs that prioritize global citizenship, empathy, and critical thinking. Ensure that schools in your community foster an understanding of global challenges and emphasize the value of cooperation over competition.

Launch Cross-Cultural Projects: Encourage collaboration between different cultural or community groups on projects that benefit everyone, such as environmental cleanups, art exhibitions, or public health campaigns. Working together on shared goals fosters a sense of unity and cooperation.

Government and Institutional Actions: Creating Supportive Frameworks

To make cultural transformation a reality on a global scale, governments and institutions must establish policies and frameworks that promote unity, inclusivity, and collective well-being. Practical steps at this level include:

Educational Reform: Governments must prioritize educational reform to foster a global perspective. Curricula should emphasize global citizenship, human rights, and shared responsibilities. By educating future generations about their role in a connected world, we can lay the foundation for global unity.

Cultural Exchange Programs: Promote cross-border cultural exchange programs that allow people from different parts of the world to live, work, and learn together. These exchanges help individuals appreciate the value of diverse experiences while recognizing our shared humanity.

Inclusive Policy Making: Ensure that policy decisions are inclusive and consider the well-being of all people, rather than prioritizing national interests. Governments must work collaboratively to develop policies that address global challenges such as climate change, pandemics, and economic inequality.

Global Governance and Representation: Establish a framework for global governance that includes fair representation for all administrative zones. This representative system should ensure that all people have a voice in decisions that affect the entire planet, promoting fairness and unity.

Promote Equality and Human Rights: Governments and institutions must protect and promote human rights, ensuring that every person, regardless of their background, is treated with dignity and respect. Protecting fundamental rights is crucial for creating an environment where cultural transformation can take place.

Grassroots Movements: Driving Change from the Bottom Up

While government actions are essential, grassroots movements play a powerful role in creating meaningful cultural change. These movements allow ordinary people to come together to advocate for global unity and influence policy changes. Practical actions for grassroots initiatives include:

Organize Campaigns for Global Citizenship: Grassroots groups can organize campaigns that emphasize the importance of adopting a global identity over narrow cultural or national identities. These campaigns can include educational initiatives, public demonstrations, and social media advocacy.

Utilize Civil Disobedience When Necessary: In cases where governments resist progress towards global unity, peaceful civil disobedience may be required. Historical examples, such as the civil rights movement in the United States or the anti-apartheid movement in South Africa, show that collective action can overcome oppressive systems and create lasting change.

Advocate for Policy Changes: Grassroots groups can put pressure on governments to enact policies that promote global unity, protect human rights, and address collective challenges. By mobilizing communities, grassroots movements can influence policy decisions at both local and global levels.

Build Networks of Solidarity: Create networks that connect like-minded individuals and organizations around the world. By working together, grassroots groups can amplify their impact and push for cultural transformation more effectively.

Leveraging Technology for Cultural Transformation

Technology is a powerful tool for connecting people and promoting cultural transformation. By leveraging the digital space, we can foster communication, understanding, and cooperation on a global scale. Practical actions in this area include:

Create Online Platforms for Dialogue: Develop

online platforms where individuals from different parts of the world can engage in dialogue, share ideas, and collaborate on global challenges. Such platforms can help build understanding and foster a shared human identity.

Promote Positive Media Narratives: Use digital media to promote stories that highlight our shared humanity and common goals. Media has the power to shape cultural attitudes, and by focusing on narratives of unity, empathy, and cooperation, we can accelerate cultural transformation.

Support Digital Education Initiatives: Utilize technology to provide access to education that promotes global citizenship, critical thinking, and empathy. Digital tools can help reach people in remote areas and ensure that everyone has the opportunity to learn and grow.

Encourage Virtual Collaboration: Use technology to enable virtual collaboration between individuals and groups across different regions. Working together on projects related to science, technology, the arts, or social development can foster a sense of connection and collective purpose.

The Road Ahead: Commitment and Collective Action

Cultural transformation is a journey that requires commitment from individuals, communities, governments, and institutions. The steps outlined in this chapter provide a roadmap for achieving a shared human identity and promoting global unity.

While the challenges are significant, the potential rewards are even greater: a world where every person has the opportunity to thrive, free from the divisions and conflicts of the past.

By embracing the practical actions outlined here, we can work together to build a future defined by peace, prosperity, and unity. It is up to each of us to play our part in making this vision a reality—whether by challenging our own biases, advocating for policy changes, participating in grassroots movements, or using technology to connect with others around the world. The path to global unity begins with the choices we make today, and by committing to cultural transformation, we can ensure a brighter future for all of humanity.

In the final chapter, we will look ahead to the future we hope to create—a future where global unity, shared prosperity, and a collective human identity guide us toward greatness. We will explore the vision of a world that thrives not despite our differences, but because we have chosen to rise above them and embrace our shared potential.

CHAPTER 13: A VISION FOR THE FUTURE: THRIVING THROUGH UNITY

As we conclude our journey through the process of cultural transformation, global governance, and practical steps towards unity, it is time to turn our gaze to the future—a future where humanity thrives as one. This chapter presents a hopeful vision of what our world could look like if we embrace the principles of global unity, shared human identity, and collective prosperity. This vision is not an unattainable dream but a real possibility if we commit to the changes we have discussed.

A World Without Borders: Freedom and Opportunity for All

Imagine a world where borders are no longer barriers that separate people but are merely administrative distinctions that help organize our shared responsibilities. In this future, individuals are free to live, work, and explore wherever they wish, without being restricted by arbitrary divisions. The freedom of movement allows people to seek opportunities, education, and a better quality of life without fear of discrimination or exclusion. Administrative zones exist to manage local governance and ensure that the needs of communities are met, but these zones are part of a borderless world where every person has the right to thrive.

This freedom of movement creates a world rich with diversity, where people from different backgrounds come together to share knowledge and experiences. It allows for a more equitable distribution of resources, as people can move to areas that provide better opportunities, and it encourages a spirit of entrepreneurship and innovation. By removing the barriers that once held us back, we create a world where everyone has the opportunity to succeed, regardless of their place of origin or social status. This new level of freedom fosters a global community where individuals are empowered to pursue their aspirations, contribute to society, and help one another achieve collective progress.

The absence of borders also means that people can respond to crises more effectively. Whether it is a natural disaster, a public health emergency, or an economic downturn, individuals and communities are no longer constrained by national boundaries when offering or receiving assistance. This interconnectedness leads to a greater sense of solidarity, as people recognize that we are all part of the same global family and that our well-being is tied to the well-being of others. By eliminating borders, we create a world where compassion, support, and mutual respect are the driving forces of our interactions.

A Global Government Representing All of Humanity

In this vision of the future, a unified global government represents the interests of all people. This government is made up of representatives elected from each administrative zone, ensuring that every voice is heard, and every community is represented. Decisions are made not based on national interests or political power, but on the collective well-being of humanity as a whole. The global council works to address the challenges that affect us all—climate change, healthcare, economic inequality, and peace—with the understanding that these issues can only be solved through collective action.

This global government operates with transparency and accountability. Citizens from every part of the world have access to information about the decisions being made and can participate in the decision-making process. Through technology and open communication, the global government ensures that every individual feels connected to the larger community and has a stake in the future of our planet.

In this future, the global government is not a distant and detached authority but an institution that actively engages with people, listens to their concerns, and works tirelessly to create policies that benefit everyone. Representatives from administrative zones are deeply rooted in their communities, understanding the unique needs and aspirations of the people they serve. This connection between governance and the governed ensures that decisions are informed by real experiences and that the voices of ordinary people are at the heart of every policy.

A Prosperous Global Economy: Fairness and Opportunity

In this future, the global economy is no longer driven by competition and exploitation but by the principles of fairness, sustainability, and shared prosperity. Global taxation replaces the old systems of national taxation, providing the resources needed to address the challenges facing humanity. The revenue collected is used to fund essential services such as healthcare, education, and infrastructure, ensuring that every person, regardless of where they live, has access to the necessities of life.

Businesses continue to play a vital role in this new world, creating jobs, driving innovation, and contributing to the global economy. However, companies operate with a sense of global responsibility, balancing the pursuit of profit with the need to contribute to the collective good. The focus is on creating value for society as a whole, rather than maximizing profits at the expense of people and the planet. Businesses are encouraged to innovate in ways that benefit both their stakeholders and the broader global community, and they are recognized and rewarded for their positive contributions to society.

The minimum living wage is a cornerstone of the global economy, providing financial stability to every working-age citizen, regardless of employment status. This wage ensures that everyone has the means to live a dignified life, pursue education, and take risks that lead to innovation and personal growth. By providing this safety net, we create a society where people are empowered to contribute in meaningful ways without the constant fear of economic insecurity.

Economic growth in this future is measured not only by traditional metrics like GDP but also by indicators of human well-being, environmental health, and social progress. The emphasis is on creating an economy that works for everyone, not just the privileged few. By focusing on sustainability and inclusivity, we ensure that economic development benefits all people and that no one is left behind. Global cooperation and the sharing of resources enable even the most disadvantaged communities to thrive, creating a world where opportunity is truly universal.

Technological Advancements: A Tool for Unity and Progress

Technology plays a central role in this future, not as a source of division or exploitation but as a tool for unity, education, and progress. Advances in technology allow for seamless communication between people across the globe, fostering understanding and collaboration. Virtual reality and augmented reality technologies bring people together in shared experiences, breaking down cultural barriers and allowing us to connect on a human level, regardless of where we are physically located.

Artificial intelligence and automation have taken over many of the mundane and repetitive tasks that once consumed our time and energy. Rather than causing unemployment and hardship, these technologies have been harnessed to improve the quality of life for all people. With basic needs met and more free time available, individuals are free to explore their passions, pursue creative endeavours, and contribute to society in ways that bring them fulfilment.

Technology also plays a key role in education, providing access to learning opportunities for people of all ages and backgrounds. Digital platforms offer courses, training programs, and educational resources that are accessible to everyone, regardless of location. This democratization of education allows individuals to develop new skills, pursue their interests, and contribute to their communities in meaningful ways. By leveraging technology for education, we create a more informed and empowered global population, ready to tackle the challenges of the future.

A Culture of Empathy, Cooperation, and Collective Identity

Perhaps the most significant change in this future is the transformation of our culture. Empathy, cooperation, and a sense of collective identity have replaced the divisive cultural markers that once defined us. People no longer see themselves as members of separate cultural, national, or religious groups, but as members of the human family. This cultural shift has led to a reduction in conflict and violence, as people recognize that harming others ultimately harms us all.

Art, music, and literature reflect this new culture of unity, celebrating the beauty of the human experience and the progress we have made together. Global celebrations bring people together to honour our shared achievements and milestones, reinforcing the idea that we are all in this together. The cultural transformation that has taken place allows us to move forward as one, with a shared purpose and a commitment to the well-being of every individual.

The shift towards a culture of empathy and cooperation is also reflected in our educational systems, which prioritize emotional intelligence, conflict resolution, and mutual respect. From a young age, children are taught the value of understanding others, working together, and contributing to the greater good. This focus on emotional and social development creates a generation of individuals who are not only skilled and knowledgeable but also compassionate and committed to making the world a better place for all.

Environmental Restoration: A Commitment to Our Planet

In this future, humanity has recognized the importance of living in harmony with the natural world. The damage done to the environment in the past has been addressed through collective action and a commitment to sustainability. Renewable energy powers our homes and industries, and ecosystems that were once on the brink of collapse have been restored to health. The air is cleaner, the oceans are free of plastic, and endangered species have been brought back from the edge of extinction.

This commitment to environmental restoration is driven by the understanding that the health of our planet is directly linked to the health of humanity. By prioritizing sustainability and recognizing our responsibility as stewards of the Earth, we have created a world where both people and the planet can thrive. The global government ensures that environmental policies are implemented fairly and effectively, with the goal of leaving a healthier planet for future generations.

Communities around the world have embraced sustainable practices, from urban farming and reforestation initiatives to waste reduction and water conservation efforts. People understand that their actions have a direct impact on the environment and are committed to making choices that protect and preserve the natural world. This collective effort has led to the revival of ecosystems, the stabilization of the climate, and the creation of a world where future generations can enjoy the beauty and abundance of nature.

The Path to Greatness: A Shared Vision for Humanity

The future we envision is not without its challenges, but it is a future worth striving for. It is a world where global unity, shared prosperity, and a collective human identity guide us towards greatness. By letting go of the divisions that have held us back and embracing our shared potential, we can create a world where every person has the opportunity to thrive, contribute, and live a meaningful life.

The path to this future begins with the choices we make today. By committing to cultural transformation, supporting global governance, and taking practical steps to promote unity, we can lay the foundation for a world that thrives not despite our differences but because we have chosen to rise above them. The journey will not be easy, but the rewards are immeasurable—a world where peace, prosperity, and human flourishing are the norm, not the exception.

Let us move forward with hope, determination, and a commitment to building a world that reflects the best of what humanity can be. Together, we can achieve greatness and create a future where every individual, every community, and every nation is part of something greater—a thriving, united human family.

EPILOGUE: THE JOURNEY BEGINS WITH US

As we stand on the threshold of a new era, we must recognize that the vision presented in this book is not just an idealistic dream—it is an achievable reality if we, as individuals, choose to make it so. The path to global unity, shared prosperity, and cultural transformation begins with each one of us. Every choice we make, every action we take, and every conversation we have brings us closer to the future we want to create.

The challenges we face are immense, and the divisions that have defined us for centuries cannot be dismantled overnight. However, history has shown us that humanity is capable of extraordinary things when we work together, guided by a shared purpose and a collective determination. The future we envision—a world without borders, a thriving global government representing all of humanity, a sustainable economy, and a culture rooted in empathy—requires us to think beyond the constraints of our current identities and embrace the idea that we are all part of the same human family.

This journey is not one that governments or institutions can take alone. It requires the participation of each individual—whether through small acts of kindness, advocacy for systemic change, or the pursuit of knowledge that helps us understand one another better. We must all play our part in shaping a world where unity triumphs over division and where our shared humanity is the foundation upon which we build a better future.

The work ahead will not always be easy. We will face obstacles, resistance, and setbacks. But we must remember that the greatest achievements in human history have always come from perseverance, from the unwavering belief that a better world is possible. The journey towards global unity and cultural transformation may take time, but every step we take in the right direction is a step worth celebrating.

Imagine the day when the divisions of the past are merely stories we tell to remind ourselves of how far we have come. Imagine a world where every individual, no matter where they were born, has the opportunity to thrive, to contribute, and to be part of something greater. Imagine a future where we are no longer defined by what separates us, but by what unites us—our shared identity as human beings.

That future is within our reach. It begins with us, here and now. Let us take the first steps together, confident in the knowledge that our efforts today will shape a world where all of humanity can thrive in unity, prosperity, and peace.

The journey to greatness has already begun. Let us walk it together.

www.ingramcontent.com/pod-product-compliance
Lightning Source LLC
Chambersburg PA
CBHW071039250726
48653CB00005B/1908